CRICKET'S
FUNNIEST JOKES

Jim Chumley

Illustrations by Robert Duncan

summersdale

CRICKET'S FUNNIEST JOKES

First published in 2009

Reprinted in 2010

This edition copyright © Summersdale Publishers Ltd, 2014

Illustrations by Roger Duncan

Summersdale Publishers Ltd
46 West Street
Chichester
West Sussex
PO19 1RP
UK

www.summersdale.com

Printed and bound in China

ISBN: 978-1-84953-512-0

Substantial discounts on bulk quantities of Summersdale books are available to corporations, professional associations and other organisations. For details contact Nicky Douglas by telephone: +44 (0) 1243 756902, fax: +44 (0) 1243 786300 or email: nicky@summersdale.com.

To...

From..

EDITOR'S NOTE

According to Douglas Adams, cricket is 'generally regarded as an incomprehensibly dull and pointless game'. Pointless maybe, but dull? This compilation of the cream of cricketing jokes begs to differ.

Anyone who happens to play the gentleman's game will strike a rich comedic vein given the unlikely characters that constitute a cricket team. Fielders have plenty of time to think up gags both on and off the pitch. As for blundering bowlers, unctuous umpires, belligerent batsmen and wise-cracking wicketkeepers – the jokes just write themselves.

These pages are packed with quotes and quips from those who know the game best – it's guaranteed to crease you up!

COMPLETELY BATTY

What does a drunk cricketer have in common with a good bat?

They're both well oiled.

There was an industrial dispute during a Test match at Lord's.

The batsmen were the first union to come out on a non-strike.

A batsman received a dressing down by the captain for being bowled out after an easy ball. 'Very well,' said the player, 'how should I have played the shot?' 'Under an assumed name,' said the wicketkeeper.

'It's a great pity you didn't take the game up sooner,' said one batsman to his older partner, who had just accidentally run him out. 'Do you mean I'd be playing first-class cricket by now?' asked his partner.
'No,' replied the batsman. 'I mean you would have already retired!'

'Has the home team scored a run yet?' enquired the spectator arriving late to the game.
'Don't ask me,' replied the man. 'I've only been watching them for the last two years.'

Two spectators were watching
the local match.
'That batsman was really late for
the first delivery,' noted one.
'He always is,' said the other. 'He's
the milkman.'

Which is the only animal you should take on to a cricket pitch?

A bat.

The captain wanted to know why
the batsman was out in the
first over.
'The ball came back very quickly,'
he explained.
'Not quite as quickly as you!'
retorted the captain.

What does an Australian cricketer look like?

Tanned, slim, holding the Ashes...

Wicketkeeper: Your bat's just like a doughnut.
Batsman: Why, because I always hit the sweet spot with it?
Wicketkeeper: No, because it seems to have a hole in it.

I CAN'T REALLY SAY I'M BATTING BADLY. I'M NOT BATTING LONG ENOUGH TO BE BATTING BADLY.

GREG CHAPPELL

The mayor was being shown
around a prison where a cricket
match was being played.
'That batsman's got talent,' he
said, 'what's he in for?'
'Hit and run!' replied the warder.

BOWLED OVER

Why did the bat make the cricketer cry?

It was made of weeping willow.

WAAAAH...

The bowler hit the batsman in the face with the ball and broke three of his teeth. The batsman went for treatment, and then bravely walked back on.

'Don't worry,' shouted the bowler. 'I'll aim for the stumps this time!'

'They asked me how I'd like to
play for England,' said John.
'"Really badly" I said.'
'I should think you could manage
that,' replied Sophie. 'All the other
players seem to.'

Bowler: I'd like to stand for a Test, please.
Captain: Sorry, we don't accept new people standing.
Bowler: How can I get a Test, then?
Captain: Beg on your knees.

BLAME IT ON THE UMPIRE

God and the Devil agreed to have a cricket match.
God thought he would win, because there were lots of Test batsmen and bowlers in Heaven.
But he overlooked the fact that all the umpires lived in Hell.

What do cricketers do when they lose their eyesight?

Become umpires.

'You can't trust anyone these days,' complained Bill, after the match.
'Why do you say that?' asked Philip.
'Well,' replied Bill, 'I bribed the umpire this afternoon and we still lost!'

'Where are your glasses?' protested the dismissed batsman angrily to the man wearing the white coat and hat. 'I think you're the one who needs glasses,' replied the man, 'but perhaps you would like to buy an ice cream?'

ALL OUT!

'Good morning's work for me,' said
the cricket-loving dentist, feeling
pleased with himself. 'I had them
all out before lunch!'

THERE'S NOTHING WRONG WITH BEING AGGRESSIVE – THE BLOKE DOWN THE OTHER END HAS A BAT, SOME PADS AND A HELMET.

SIMON JONES

The streaker ran through the
ladies' changing room and
disappeared out of the door.
'Was that a regular member?'
asked one, shocked.
'A little on the small side, if you
ask me,' replied another.

The young man got permission to take the day off so he could be at his father's funeral. His boss was furious to see the man at the local cricket match that very afternoon. When he arrived the score was 0 for 6.

'This doesn't look like your father's funeral to me!' fumed the boss.

'I wouldn't be too sure,' the man gulped, 'he's next up to bat!'

'I had five catches dropped this
afternoon,' complained
the bowler.
'True,' replied his skipper. 'But
the spectators aren't expected to
catch them from all the way up in
the stands!'

I BOWL SO SLOWLY
THAT IF, AFTER I HAVE DELIVERED THE BALL, I DON'T LIKE THE LOOK OF IT, I CAN RUN AFTER IT AND BRING IT BACK.

J. M. BARRIE

CREASING UP

Why do cricketers look weather-beaten?

Because rain always stops play.

THERE WAS A SLIGHT INTERRUPTION THERE FOR ATHLETICS.

RICHIE BENAUD, REFERRING TO A STREAKER AT LORD'S

'Now, don't forget to get behind
the ball,' said the coach to
the boy.
'But it's round!' the boy exclaimed.
'How do you tell which is the front
and which is the back?'

A fielder on the boundary ran to make a catch deep in the field, but he stumbled and the ball fell through his hands.

'I probably could have caught that quite easily in my mouth,' jeered a spectator.

'If my mouth was as enormous as yours, I probably could have done too,' snapped the fielder.

One cricketer asked another,
'Does your village boast a
cricket team?'
'We have a team,' replied the
other. 'But I wouldn't say it was
anything to boast about!'

The cricket team were losing
very heavily and couldn't decide
which batsman to play next.
'Shall we bring out our hooker?'
asked one player.
'The game's not over yet, young
man, we'll have none of that,'
replied the captain.

The wicketkeeper had a bad day, dropping eight catches. What's more, he felt a bit under the weather. 'I've got a cold coming on,' he muttered.

'Well, it makes a change that you've been able to catch something,' grumbled the bowler.

ODDBALLS

I DON'T GO AS FAR AS THAT ON MY HOLIDAYS.

ANONYMOUS BOWLER, COMMENTING ON THE LENGTH OF BOB WILLIS'S RUN-UP

Caught out early, the batsman made his way to the pavilion for his lunch of fish and chips. 'This batter's terrible,' he grimaced. The chef scowled back, 'Look who's talking!'

The police arrived at the match. 'We've had a report of an individual acting suspiciously, loitering around without doing anything,' said the sergeant. 'Oh yes, he's over there,' replied the groundsman, pointing to the England fielder.

Who scores a hat-trick?

A bowler, of course!

SIMPLY NOT CRICKET

THE ENGLISH ARE NOT VERY SPIRITUAL PEOPLE, SO THEY INVENTED CRICKET TO GIVE THEM SOME IDEA OF ETERNITY.

G. B. SHAW

Bowler: I've got a brilliant idea for improving our team.

Captain: Excellent! When will you be leaving?

The batsman, proud of his sporting prowess, was keen to impress his mother-in-law sitting in the stands. Taking his position on the crease, he turned to the wicketkeeper and said, 'I plan to really belt this one. My mother-in-law is over there.' 'Don't be daft,' replied the wicketkeeper. 'You'll never hit her at this distance!'

I COULDN'T BAT FOR THE LENGTH OF TIME REQUIRED TO SCORE 500. I'D GET BORED AND FALL OVER.

DENNIS COMPTON

A bout of torrential rain had cast doubts on whether a crucial Test match would take place. The ground was soaked, but they decided to play anyway. The home captain won the toss and, after a moment's thought, exclaimed, 'Right then – we'll have the shallow end.'

Why did the cricket team sack the committee at their village show?

They said it was time to take charge of their own fete.

'I'm surprised the spectators don't riot out of boredom!' said one bowler to the other during the dull match.
'Yes, but it's difficult to shout and yawn at the same time,' replied his friend.

When do Sussex batsmen display their best footwork?

When they walk back to the pavilion.

WRONG-FOOTED

I JUST WANT TO GET INTO THE MIDDLE AND GET THE RIGHT SORT OF RUNS.

ROBIN SMITH, ON SUFFERING FROM DIARRHOEA WHILE ON TOUR IN INDIA

'If W. G. Grace were here today I wonder how he would play in this Twenty20 cricket match?'

'Not very well I shouldn't think. He'd be over one hundred and fifty years old!'

'If the fans start haranguing me for my autograph,' said the arrogant county player, 'I pretend that I don't play any more.' Said the journalist under his breath, 'I'm not sure you have to pretend.'

'Where's your scoreboard?' asked
the visiting captain.
'Over there,' said the home bowler,
pointing to a strapping boxer
standing by the pavilion.
'What if we don't agree with
his scoring?' asked the
visiting captain.
'You can take it up with him
afterwards,' offered the
local bowler.

Which cricket team is most sensibly dressed for cold weather?

The Vest Indies.

'How can I improve my batting?'
'You need to play with more spirit, son.'
'I've had three vodkas and a gin already – I won't be able to see the ball if I have any more.'

'Do you know the statistics for
last season?' a cricketer asked
at his club's annual
general meeting.
'Well, as far as I know, it was 298
gallons of beer in 50 pubs.'

DOWN BUT NOT OUT

Patient: Doctor, I'm feeling just like an umpire.

Doctor: Don't be silly. There must be someone somewhere who likes you!

One cricketer to another:
'That doctor doesn't know what
he's talking about.'
'What did he say?'
'He told me I've got tennis elbow!'

Patient: Doctor, I've got a cricket bat in my ear!
Doctor: How's that?
Patient: Don't start that again!

Batsman: My doctor has told me I can't play cricket.

Captain: I didn't know he knew you so well!

The umpire bent his arm and
shouted, 'One short.'
'Cheeky!' replied the batsman.
'How did you know?'

Patient: Doctor, I keep seeing ducks before my eyes.
Doctor: Have you seen an optician?
Patient: No, just ducks.

HIT AND MRS

'What do you think about
Joan going off with the
cricket coach?'

'I didn't know she
could drive.'

A batsman saw his friend moping around behind the pavilion at the end of a match and asked him why he looked so despondent.
'My wife has told me she wants a divorce,' he said glumly.
'Really?' enquired his friend, 'On what grounds?'
'Oh, I'm not sure; it could be Headingley, Lord's, Edgbaston...'

'I've just got a new cricket bat
for my husband.'

'Wow, what a great swap!'

'Doctor, I need something to help my husband rest before his big match.'
'Here are some sleeping pills. They should do the trick.'
'What's the dosage?'
'You just swallow half of them this evening and he'll be right as rain in the morning.'

PITCHES ARE LIKE WIVES – YOU CAN NEVER TELL HOW THEY'RE GOING TO TURN OUT.

LEONARD HUTTON

Fred always played cricket on Sunday. This troubled his wife, so she asked the vicar whether it was a sin to play on Sunday. 'It's not a sin,' replied the vicar. 'The way he plays, it's a crime!'

Smith took his wife to a cricket match and, although bored, she sat patiently through the first innings. During the second, a batsman made a wild hook and cleared the ball from the grounds. 'Thank goodness they got rid of it,' said Smith's wife, 'Now we can all go home.'

If you're interested in finding out more
about our books, find us on Facebook at
Summersdale Publishers and follow us
on Twitter at @Summersdale.

www.summersdale.com